Everybody Toots!

Justine Avery

Naday Meldova

SUTEKI
CREATIVE

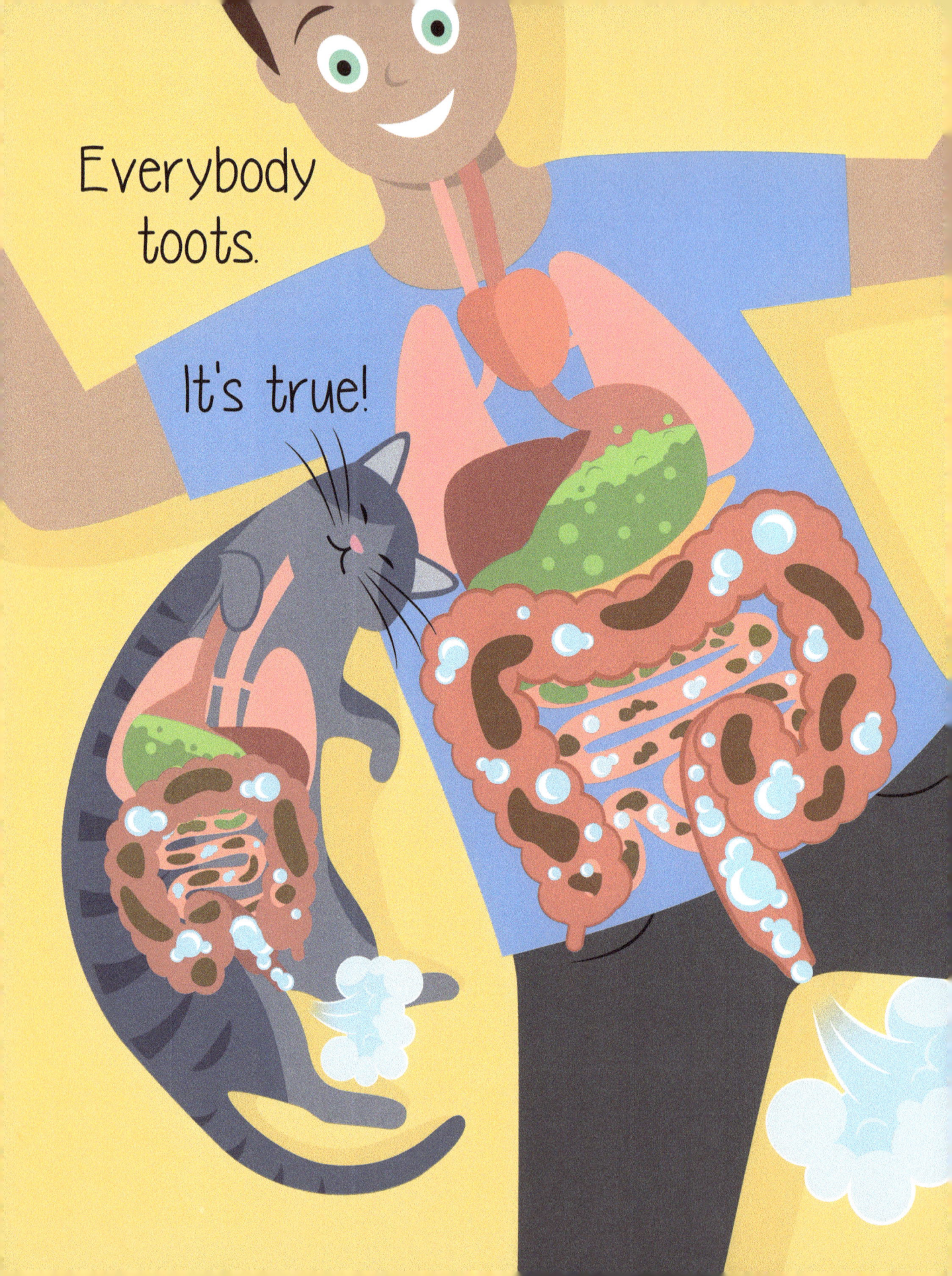

Everybody toots.

It's true!

EVERY family...

The school principal, every headmistress, and the prime minister definitely toot.

Rock stars and dog walkers, taxi drivers and toy makers... they all need to toot.

Movie stars and mountain climbers, zoo keepers and street sweepers... Each and every one of them really does toot!

And they toot

a lot.

Every single day.

Just like ALL of us do.

Some itty bitty insects toot.
And the tiniest mouse.
And whales bigger than your house!

So do most farm animals...

all the sea mammals, and frogs, of course.

And snakes toot. And tigers and alligators and the old mighty dinosaurs!

Nearly every creature on this planet toots.

Nearly every BODY on the planet toots.

Our toots are in the air.

Our toots are in the sea.

Our toots are practically

EVERYWHERE!

And now, get ready... for the biggest confession of all.

For the child in all of us,
may we never grow too old
to see all the silliness in life.
—J.A.

My grandfather
was an artist
and instilled in me
the love of drawing.
—N.M.

Justine Avery is an award-winning author who loves writing stories for all sorts of readers. She was born in America but grew up—and is still growing up—all over the world as a natural explorer with a curiosity for all things. She's jumped out of airplanes, off of very high bridges, and into shark-infested waters—to name a few adventures. And books are her favorite adventures of all.

Naday Meldova is an artist who graduated from art school in Tula, Russia. She's been illustrating for years, and this is her favorite job!

First published 2021 by Suteki Creative

First Edition

Copyright © 2021 Justine Avery
Illustrated by Naday Meldova
All rights reserved.

In accordance with international copyright law, this publication, in full or in part, may not be scanned, copied, stored in a retrieval system, duplicated, reproduced, uploaded, transmitted, resold, or distributed online or offline—in any form or by any means—without prior, explicit permission of the author.

But *please do*… lend this book freely! It's *yours*—you own it. So, pass it on, trade it in, exchange it with and recommend it to other readers. Books are the very best gifts.

ISBN: 978-1-63882-231-8
ISBN: 978-1-63882-229-5 (ebook)
ISBN: 978-1-63882-232-5 (hardcover)
ISBN: 978-1-63882-234-9 (audio book)